magic

a *flowmotion*™ title

magic

colin francome

Sterling Publishing Co., Inc.
New York

Created and conceived by
Axis Publishing Limited
8c Accommodation Road
London NW11 8ED
www.axispublishing.co.uk

Creative Director: Siân Keogh
Managing Editor: Brian Burns
Project Designer: Sean Keogh
Project Editor: Madeleine Jennings
Production Manager: Sue Bayliss
Photographer: Mike Good

Library of Congress Cataloging-in-Publication
Data Available

10 9 8 7 6 5 4 3 2 1

Published in 2002 by Sterling Publishing Co., Inc.
387 Park Avenue South, New York, NY 10016
Text and images © Axis Publishing Limited 2002
Distributed in Canada by Sterling Publishing
C/o Canadian Manda Group,
One Atlantic Avenue, Suite 105
Toronto, Ontario, M6K 3E7, Canada

Separation by
United Graphics Pte Limited
Printed and bound by
Star Standard (Pte) Limited

Sterling ISBN 0–8069–9376–6

a *flowmotion*™ title

magic

contents

introduction   **6**

tricks with playing cards   **14**

tricks with rope   **34**

tabletop magic   **52**

index   **94**

ten reasons to do magic

● **MAGIC CAN HELP IN ALL PARTS OF LIFE** When my daughter was preparing for her travels, I used magic techniques to help her hide her valuables. Principles that magicians use can help you to remember people's names and phone numbers.

● **MAGIC IS FUN** It is easy to take life too seriously. Magic is ideal for adding the fun element to life. It is lighthearted compared to many leisure activities.

● **MAGIC IS SOCIABLE** Performing magic can be a singular activity, but many derive great pleasure from working with others. You can teach each other new tricks, monitor each other's performance, and find ways to improve. A number of tricks require cooperation. Magic can also be a way of meeting new people. There are magic clubs and conventions, both in this country and abroad.

● **MAGIC IS INTERNATIONAL** Wherever you go in the world and whatever language is spoken, people will always appreciate the skill that is required to perform magic tricks.

● **MAGICIANS CAN ENTERTAIN** Even if you can only do a few tricks, you can entertain children, who always find magic very amusing.

● **MAGIC CAN BE DONE AT ANY TIME** If you experience a delay in catching an airplane or train, fill the time by improving your skills. At the same time, you may be helping to cheer other people up.

● **SELF-IMPROVEMENT** People obtain immense satisfaction when they improve their own performance and progress with difficult tricks. Some magic tricks use numbers, which can help young people develop their numerical skills. Other tricks develop spacial awareness.

● **MAGIC IS NOT NECESSARILY EXPENSIVE** In this book we show you many magic tricks that you can do with everyday objects.

● **MAGIC CAN BE INVENTIVE** Once you have learned what others have been able to achieve, you can develop a few ideas.

● **MAGIC CAN IMPROVE CONCENTRATION AND DEXTERITY** Some tricks require great attention to perform.

PERFORMANCE TIPS FOR YOUNG MAGICIANS

In general, do not repeat a trick, because the surprise will have gone. It is much better to move on to something else that the audience will find just as enjoyable.

Practice your tricks to make sure you can do them perfectly. It is probably a good idea not to try too many different tricks at once. Someone commented that one difference between an amateur magician and a professional one is that the professional performs a few tricks for many people, while an amateur performs many tricks for a few people.

Watch other magicians live or on television to enjoy their show and learn from their presentation.

When watching other magicians, be supportive of their performances, especially if you know the trick. This will help improve the status of magic.

Do not reveal how tricks are performed outside the recognized ways of passing on information – through books or articles, or at special lectures or videos for magicians.

Look cheerful when you are performing. If it is evident you are having a good time, it is more likely that everyone else will, too.

Do not perform for too long. It is better to leave your audience wanting more.

prediction tricks

People have always wanted to predict the future, and magicians can help to do this.

The sweet trick

Also called The Candy I Did Not Like, this is a simple but very effective number trick. To perform it, you need to place six different colored hard candies in a row on a table in front of you. Make sure the red candy is third in the line. Explain to your audience that there is one kind of candy you do not like, and ask a volunteer to choose a number between one and six. No matter what number they choose, it will always lead to the red candy. This is achieved by:

1. Spelling out the letters O N E to land on the red.
2. Spelling out the letters T W O to land on the red.
3. Counting out "one, two, three" to land on the red.
4. Spelling out the letters F O U R, starting at the other end, to land on the red.
5. Spelling out the letters F I V E, starting at the other end, to land on the red.
6. Spelling out the letters S I X to land on the red.

Now surprise your audience by pouring out lots of red candies from a container on the table.

Fun with letters

Tell your audience that you are going to spell out the numbers of a complete suit of cards, and each time you say a letter, you are going to take the top card and place it on the bottom. After you have spelled the word ACE, the fourth card is seen to be the Ace and is removed from the deck. The next number, TWO, is spelled out, and after the O, the card two is shown and removed. This process continues until only the King is left in the hand. This trick simply depends on the order of the cards. The 13 cards should be set out as follows:

3, 8, 7, Ace, Queen, 6, 4, 2, Jack, King, 10, 9, 5.

Once you have set out this order, the trick works by itself.

palms and sleights

There are a number of basic skills that magicians use when performing tricks, and they usually involve concealing an object so the audience thinks it has disappeared into thin air. The ones shown here are used in many of the tricks described in the book, so practice them well.

The size and shape of sponge balls make them easy to conceal and manipulate during tricks.

PALMING A COIN

1 From the front, the hand looks empty. The position of the hand also seems quite natural.

2 The coin is actually hidden by the little finger. Direct the audience's attention elsewhere.

PALMING A BALL

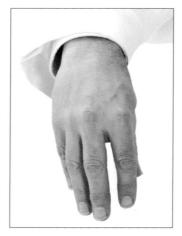

1 The hand appears insignificant. Looking and pointing away from the hand will emphasize this.

2 The view from the back shows the ball being lightly held in the center of your palm without using your fingers.

LAPPING

PALMING A CARD

1 Your hand needs to be larger than the card. Children may need to use a miniature deck of cards.

2 The card is removed. Your eyes and words should direct the audience's attention to the deck.

If you are sitting at a table, you can direct the audience's attention to the visible action on top of the table, while quietly dropping items into your lap.

3 The hand concealing the card is moved away without being the object of the audience's attention.

4 If the hand were turned over, it would show the concealed card cupped in your palm.

the french drop

The French drop is a good technique for making a coin disappear, as it travels from one hand to another. Use your eyes to follow the coin from one hand to another, which will help misdirect the audience from the coin's true position. You should also allow a bit of time to pass between performing the French Drop and revealing to the audience that the coin has vanished; otherwise, you might arouse suspicion. Let the hand that is holding the coin drop to your side as you look at the other hand, which is supposedly holding the coin.

1 Hold the coin between the thumb and index finger of your left hand. Draw the audience's attention toward it.

2 When your right hand is covering the coin, lift your left thumb so it drops into your left palm.

3 Tell the audience you have taken the coin into your right hand.

4 Curl your right hand up into a fist to exaggerate the swap.

5 Point at your right hand to distract your audience from the reality.

go with the flow

The special created *Flowmotion* images used in this book allow you to see the whole of each magic trick – not just selected highlights. We have shown each trick as it is performed to an audience, and reveal afterward the secrets of how it is done. Each of the image sequences flows across the page from left to right.

Each magic trick routine is carefully explained with detailed captions beneath the images. An additional layer of information underneath the captions highlights the key moves of each trick. The key to performing magic well is to practice frequently. With lots of different tricks to choose from, you will soon become expert at one, if not more.

four burglars | 17

four burglars *tricks with playing cards*

The name of this fun card trick originates from the short story that you tell while performing it.

the secret

● Show the audience a deck of cards. Tell them you are going to pick up four cards from the top of the deck, which are all Jacks. Fan out the four Jacks in your right hand.

● Begin the story: Once upon a time there were four burglars (place the cards back on top of the deck in front of you). They each decided to rob a different floor of a house.

● The first went to the first floor (cut the deck low down, take the top card, and put it there). The second went to the second floor (cut the deck a little higher up, take the card at the top of the pile, and put it there).

● The third burglar went to the third floor (do the same thing again). The last burglar decided to stay on top to act as lookout (put the last card on top of pile). Suddenly, they heard a police car wailing in the background.

● They rushed to the roof the house to escape down the fire escape. (At this point, bang your hand dramatically on the pack.)

● Now, pick up the first card to reveal a Jack. To your audience's amazement, when you pick up the next card it will be another Jack.

● Pick up the next two cards from the top of the deck, which will also be Jacks. In one hand, show off to your audience the four "burglars."

● Underneath the top three cards of the deck are the four Jacks. Leave the last Jack slightly askew so you can pick up the first seven cards easily from the top of the deck. Hide the first three cards behind the last fanned out Jack.

■ show the four Jacks ▶ put Jacks back on deck ▶ insert cards into deck ▶ ▶ reveal the top card ■ pick up seven cards

■ This indicates the beginning or end of a sequence, where there is no movement.

▶ This indicates continued movement in the sequence.

tricks with playing cards

four burglars

tricks with playing cards

The name of this fun card trick originates from the short story that
you tell while performing it.

● Show the audience a deck of cards.
Tell them you are going to pick up
four cards from the top of the deck,
which are all Jacks. Fan out the four
Jacks in your right hand.

● Begin the story: Once upon a time
there were four burglars (place the
cards back on top of the deck in front
of you). They each decided to rob a
different floor of a house.

● The first went to the first floor (cut
the deck low down, take the top card,
and put it there). The second went to
the second floor (cut the deck a little
higher up, take the card at the top of
the pile, and put it there).

● The third burglar went to the third
floor (do the same thing again). The
last burglar decided to stay on top to
act as lookout (put the last card on
top of pile). Suddenly, they heard a
police car wailing in the background.

the secret

● They rushed to the roof the house to escape down the fire escape. (At this point, bang your hand dramatically on the pack.)

● Now, pick up the first card to reveal a Jack. To your audience's amazement, when you pick up the next card it will be another Jack.

● Pick up the next two cards from the top of the deck, which will also be Jacks. In one hand, show off to your audience the four "burglars."

● Underneath the top three cards of the deck are the four Jacks. Leave the last Jack slightly askew so you can pick up the first seven cards easily from the top of the deck. Hide the first three cards behind the last fanned out Jack.

suspended cards playing cards

As the name suggests, this is a trick where a number of cards are magically suspended from your hand. When the magic word is spoken, the cards magically drop down.

● Explain to your audience that you are going to perform an amazing, gravity-defying card trick. Fan out a deck of cards in one hand and show them to your audience.

● Straighten up the deck; then pick up eight or so cards from the top of the deck with your left hand.

● Place the remaining deck to one side. Now tell your audience you are going to spread the chosen cards, face up, in your right hand.

● Continue chatting to your audience while you rearrange the cards in the palm of your right hand.

the secret

- The spread of cards should cover your whole hand. Slowly raise up your hand, then turn it so the palm is facing downwards.

- Your audience will be amazed, as the cards stay magically stuck to your hand!

- Now, say a magic word, such as "release," and watch the cards fall to the table.

- One card has a small tab cut out of its middle, which lets you hold the card upside down. Put this card down first, holding the tab between your index and second finger. Arrange the other cards to lie under this card.

raise your hand ▶ **let the cards drop** ▶ ■

turn the card over *playing cards*

This is a trick where a card magically turns over. It is a good one to perform in front of young children as you can ask for a volunteer to come and assist you.

● As you introduce your trick to the audience, place a deck of cards face down on the table in front of you.

● Pick up the deck in one hand. Keep the cards face down towards the table while you use your other hand to fan them out. Ask a volunteer to pick a card from your fanned hand.

● Tell your volunteer to look at the chosen card (in this instance, it is the King of Clubs). Make eye contact and ask "can you remember your card?" Close the deck, then quickly and surreptitiously turn the deck over.

● Ask your helper to place the card back in the closed deck. All the while, maintain eye contact and continue to chat about having a memory good enough to remember the chosen card.

the secrets

● Now tap the top of the deck and say a magic word as you begin to fan the deck out in your hands.

● To the audience's and your participant's amazement, the chosen card will appear face up in the fan. Declare it magic!

● In the beginning, make sure you arrange the deck so that the card at the bottom is facing upward. When you fan the pack out, don't reveal the last, upturned card.

● At this point, all the cards except the top one are face upward. When your helper looks you in the eye, turn the deck back over again in a swift movement that will not attract any attention.

In this trick, a helper magically cuts the cards to Aces. Practice handling a deck of cards to appear confident in front of your audience.

- Display a deck of cards on the table in front of you. Although I am shown performing this trick, you can ask a volunteer from the audience to come and perform the moves for you.

- Pick up roughly three quarters of the deck and move them to your left (or ask your volunteer to do this).

- Drop a third of this pile onto the table next to the original and repeat once more until the whole deck is now divided roughly into four.

- Pick up the first pile (farthest to your right), and deal the first three cards from the top of the pile to the bottom.

the secret

● Now take the next three cards from the top of the same pile you are holding, and place each of them on top of the other three piles of cards.

● When you have finished, put that pile of cards down and pick up the next pile of cards. Do the same thing: put the top three to the bottom, and then put the next three on top of each of the piles on the table.

● Now deal the next three cards onto the top of the other pack. When you reveal the top card of each pile, they will all show an Ace and your audience will be completely baffled!

● Arrange the deck of cards beforehand so the four Aces are at the top of the pile. After you cut the deck into four, make sure the pile with the Aces on top is the last to be dealt.

▶ **deal the next two piles** ▶ **reveal the four aces** ■

forcing a card

This is one of the most important magic skills. The volunteer thinks he or she is choosing a card completely of their choice, but it is actually the one the magician wants to be chosen! Perform the card force well and you will be able to do a whole host of card tricks!

● Present the audience a deck of cards. Prepare the deck beforehand so that the Queen of Hearts, the card you are about to force, is the card on the top of the pile.

● Ask a member of the audience to help you cut the deck. Say, "pick up a third of the deck; turn it over and place it face up, back on the deck again."

● Now ask your volunteer to pick up two thirds of the deck and do the same thing, turning them face up back on the deck.

● Use both hands to fan the deck of cards out in front of you, so the audience can see all the cards.

● Ask your volunteer to pick out the first card that is face down and show it to the rest of the audience, but not to you. Say "memorize the card."

● Because you have prepared the deck beforehand—with the Queen of Hearts on the top—you know that the first card face down will be the Queen of Hearts.

● So, before you start the trick, place another Queen of Hearts in your jacket pocket. Once your volunteer has chosen the forced card, you can pull the identical card out of your pocket and surprise your volunteer!

● For a really professional touch, buy a silk handkerchief displaying a Queen of Hearts picture, and pull this from you pocket instead!

pick out a card   ▶   ▶   ▶   **match the forced card**   ■

appearing and disappearing cards

There is one surprise after another in this trick! First of all, four cards appear.

Then two disappear and reappear in an empty box.

● Tell the audience you have a magic box in front of you.

● Take the lid off and show the inside of the box to the audience. Put the box back down in front of you, and put the lid back on.

● Take the lid off again and pull out four cards that have magically appeared inside the box. In this case, we have used the Ace and King of Clubs, and the Ace and King of Diamonds.

● Put the cards back into the box, then place the lid on top. Tap the top of the box and say a magic word.

● Take off the lid again and this time pull out two cards—the Ace of Clubs and King of Diamonds.

● Place the cards to one side, then lift up the empty box to show there are no extra cards inside the box.

● Put the box back down in front of you again and replace the lid.

● When you take off the lid this time, pull out the two remaining cards—the Ace of Diamonds and King of Clubs. Show the audience that the box is completely empty.

appearing and disappearing cards — the secrets

Glue together some cards so that four (the Ace and King of Clubs and the Ace and King of Diamonds) appear fanned out on one side, and only two (the Ace of Clubs and the King of Diamonds) appear on the reverse. Hide another Ace of Diamonds and a King of Clubs inside a secret sleeve on the underside of the lid.

● Set up the box with the lid slightly askew. Carefully balance the glued set of cards on the edge of the box underneath the lid.

● When you pick up the lid, pick up the glued set of cards as well. As you put the lid back down onto the box, release your grip so the cards drop into the box.

● When you take the lid off again, pull out the glued set of cards, making sure you show to the audience the side that has four cards fanned out. Put them back into the box and cover with the lid.

balance glued cards on edge ▶   ▶ **show four cards** ▶

● When you lift out the cards again, show the other side so the audience thinks you are showing only two of the original four cards. Carefully put the cards to the side, making sure the audience cannot see they are glued.

● Underneath the inside of the lid is a secret sleeve where you have hidden an extra Ace of Diamonds and King of Clubs. Take the lid off and put it down beside you, without showing its underside.

● As you put the lid back on, turn the lid towards you so the top of it is facing towards your audience. At the same time, use your thumbs to loosen the two cards from their secret sleeve.

● When you open the lid, you will be able to pick up what the audience thinks is the two remaining cards from the four originally shown.

show two cards ▶ **release hidden cards** ▶

the rising card

tricks with playing cards

In this trick, the card that your volunteer has chosen magically rises from the deck!

● Present a deck of cards in one hand to your audience. Fan out the deck with both hands and ask a volunteer to pick out a card.

● The card chosen should be hidden from your view, but shown to the audience. In this case, the card chosen is the Jack of Hearts.

● Straighten up the deck and now ask your volunteer to put the chosen card back into the middle of the pack.

● Pick up the deck with your left hand and gradually drop them into your right hand. Tell your volunteer to place the card back somewhere into the pile in your right hand.

pick out a card ▶   ▶ **return card to deck**   ▶   ▶

● When the card has been placed back into the deck, drop the rest of the cards from your left hand back down onto the pack.

● To perform this trick to its best effect, stand a good distance away from the audience.

● Transfer the deck of cards to your right hand and hold them up to the audience. The face of the deck should be showing toward the audience.

● To the audience's delight, the chosen card then magically rises from the deck.

drop cards on top ▶ **hold up deck** ▶ **raise chosen card** ◼

the rising card—the secrets

The concept behind this trick is very simple. However, to perform it well, you need nimble fingers and a lot of practice beforehand.

● When you ask the volunteer to put the chosen card back into the deck, separate the deck with both hands.

● Drop the top half of the deck onto the bottom half (which has the chosen card on top of it) at an angle of about 30 degrees.

● The top half of the deck now juts out slightly from the bottom half of the pack.

● Hold your volunteer's gaze as you lift the cards at the point where they jut out and quickly transfer them to the bottom of the pile. The chosen card will now be on the top.

● Arrange the deck of cards in your right hand so you can display them face forward toward the audience.

● Your thumb should be on one side of the pack and your first two fingers behind the pack.

● Use your index finger to slowly push the last card—the chosen card— up from the rest of the deck.

● Take your left hand over and pull out the levitated card from behind and present it to your audience.

show cards face forward   ▷   ▷   **raise the card**   ▷   **present the card**   ■

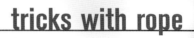

tricks with rope

threading a needle *rope*

Rope tricks are similar to juggling acts because they require a lot of swift hand and arm movement. They are great fun to perform, but practice them well beforehand. For this trick you will need a piece of rope about 3 feet long. A brightly colored one will be easier for your audience to see.

● Hold the ends of the rope in both hands out in front of you and ask your audience, "Do you have trouble threading a needle?"

● Hold up your left thumb and arrange the rope so about a quarter is draped over your thumb toward the audience. The rest dangles between your hand and chest.

● Wind the long piece under and over your thumb, pulling it back toward your chest. Work from the joint of your thumb and hand toward the tip of your thumb. Near the end of your thumb, make a large loop.

● Hold the loop in place with your thumb against your index finger. Make sure the audience can see it above your hand. The end of the rope should make up the side of loop farthest from your wrist.

● Tell your audience that no matter how bad your aim, you still manage to thread the loop. Pick up the rope end that is closest to your wrist, not the one you have been winding around, and slide it behind your thumb.

● Aim to miss the loop by going to its right. As you pull the end toward the audience, the rope will automatically thread through the loop. Pull it out and do it again.

● The third time, tie a knot at the end of the rope you are feeding through toward the audience.

● As it threads through the loop again, pull back on it to show the knot is genuine and doesn't come out. Enjoy yourself as your audience remains baffled!

▶ **intentionally miss the loop** ▶ **tie a knot at the end** ▶ **ask the audience to try it** ■

self-tying knots

Introduce these two tricks to your audience as "the knot you tie in a piece of rope without letting go of the ends." The first trick is much easier than the second.

● Lay a long piece of rope out on the table in front you. Fold your arms, left over right.

● Lean forward, toward your left, to pick up that end of the rope, holding it over the outside of your arm.

● Next lean forward, toward your right, to pick up the other rope end, holding it on the inside of your arm.

● As you unravel your arms, making sure your left hand goes under the right hand and the rope it is holding, you will automatically pull the rope into a knot. Practice it so you can do it fast to greater effect.

■ **fold your arms** ▶ **lean forward to left** ▶ **lean forward to right** ▶ **unravel your arms** ■

the secret

● Hold the rope ends with thumb and index finger. Take the rope end in your right hand over the left hand, out towards the audience. Bring it down under the loop created between your left fingers and left wrist.

● Feed the rope end through the two pieces of rope hanging on the sides of your left wrist, passing your right hand under your left wrist. Now flex your right wrist back and feed the rope toward you under your left hand.

● Pull your hands slightly apart so the inside of your wrists are facing each other. Now flick your wrists so your fingers face down to the floor, and pull the hands apart. You will have produced a knot, but others won't.

● As you flick, change your right-hand grip so you let go of the end of the rope and hold onto the rope closest to the outside edge of your palm. This is what creates the knot. Others who try this will be baffled!

■ **form a complicated knot** ▶ ▶ **flick the wrists** ■ **change your grip** ■

quick-release ring *tricks with rope*

Showmanship plays a big part in this trick. Anyone who performs it will soon realize that the knot tied around the ring is designed to slip off easily. Making it look difficult is what creates the magic.

● To perform this trick, you will need a long piece of rope and a solid ring, which can be purchased at your local hardware store. The smaller the ring, the easier it will be to slip off the knot.

● Make a loop in the middle of the rope, and place that over the ring, up toward its center. Next, bring the rope ends up over the ring and through the loop.

● Ask two volunteers from the audience to come up and hold the rope ends on each side so that the ring is suspended in front of you.

● Now pull out a large and heavy piece of cloth, such as a napkin, from your pocket. Place it evenly over the ring so that both ends of the napkin meet and the ring is hidden from sight.

the secrets

Behind the scenes, use both hands to slip the rope off the ring, gradually and without too much tugging.

● Keep your gaze focused on your audience as you place your hands beneath the napkin.

● In a few seconds you should be able to slip the knot quickly off the ring. Unveil the knotless ring to the audience and declare it magic!

● With the knot at the top of the ring, you will need to pull the two pieces of rope that make up the knot down each side of the ring.

● Concentrate on controlling the tension of the rope on the ring. If you work too fast, the ring might "pop up" and slip out of your hands.

place hands beneath cloth ▶ **release knot** ■ **slide the rope down the side** ▶ **control the tension** ■

it's a snip 1 *with rope*

An old favorite of many magicians, this trick is also known as cut and restored rope because it involves a piece of rope being cut into two halves, and then magically restored back into one.

- Present to your audience a long piece of rope. Explain that it is a bit too long, so you need to cut it.

- Separate the rope ends so you can hold it up in front of you and show the audience that it is one long, continuous piece of rope. Then bring the two ends together.

- Hold the two ends in one hand between your palm and your thumb. Your palm should be facing toward your chest and your thumb obscured from the audience's view. Flip the ends of the rope over the top of your hand.

- Now use your other hand to pick up the loop created at the bottom of the rope.

● Bring the loop up past the top of your hand for your audience to see. Ask your assistant to place some scissors in your other hand, then cut the loop so your audience can clearly see four ends of the rope.

● Adjust the grip on your thumb so that you drop the two ends you were originally holding. Tell your audience you now have two pieces of rope.

● Tell your audience you are now going to tie the two ends of the rope together.

● If you like, you can even ask a member of the audience to come up and do it. Hold up the knot for everyone to see.

it's a snip 2 *with rope*

This trick requires some manual dexterity, so practice holding the rope between your thumb and palm, dropping the rope ends on command, and tying ends with one knot before you perform it.

● Once you have shown the audience the two pieces of rope tied together in the middle, begin to wind the rope up and around your hand.

● Keep your left hand on the rope, making sure the top of your left hand is facing the audience.

● Keeping the fingers of your left hand tightly closed, unravel the rope to the audience.

● Hold the rope ends with your thumbs and index fingers to show how it has been restored magically back into one piece again.

the secrets

● When you tell your audience that you are going to cut the piece of rope in half, bring the middle (loop) of the rope up and behind the palm of your right hand.

● When it is behind your hand, out of the audience's view, put your fingers under the loop to pick up the piece of rope held against your thumb farthest to your left. Bring that up and over the top of your hand instead.

● The audience thinks you cut the middle of the rope, but you actually only cut a bit off one end of the rope. Once cut, drop the two outer ends of the rope. From the front, you appear to be holding two equal-length ropes.

● You only tie the small piece of rope around the middle of the long piece. When you wind the rope, put your left hand on the knot, slide it off, and conceal it from the audience's view, into your palm.

pick up middle ▶ **change your grip** ▶ **cut and drop ends** ▶ **hide knot in one hand** ◼

tricks with rope

Also known as The Professor's Nightmare, this winning rope trick requires practice! You will need three pieces of rope cut accurately to size. The longest should be 3 feet (92 cm), the middle 21.5 inches (55 cm), and the shortest 10.5 inches (27 cm).

● Hold up three pieces of rope in one hand, and tell your audience that you have a daddy elephant's trunk, a mommy elephant's trunk, and a baby elephant's trunk. At the same time, wiggle the corresponding sized ropes.

● Continue storytelling..."When they went to the watering hole, the mommy elephant's trunk was the right length, but the daddy elephant's trunk was too long and the baby elephant's trunk was too short..."

● "...so the mommy elephant had to feed the baby elephant and clean the daddy elephant's trunk. That night, when they went to sleep, all the elephants hung their trunks up on a nearby branch."

● At this point, pick up the dangling rope ends, one by one, and put them all into your right hand. The audience should be able to see six rope ends peeking out from above your palm.

● Continue with..."The mommy elephant had a dream that the baby elephant's trunk grew and the daddy elephant's shrunk, so the trunks were all the same size." At this point, let three rope ends dangle down.

● The audience should now see three even pieces of rope dangling from your palm. Continue with the story..."And the mommy elephant was very happy because she didn't have to do extra work at the watering hole."

● Show one piece of rope and transfer it to your right hand.

the three elephants 2

● Pass the second rope over to your right hand and then the third. Place one piece of rope over your shoulder and tie the other two equal lengths together.

● Now continue on with the story. "The elephants decided to go to a new watering hole As they travelled through the jungle, they decided to link up trunks so they wouldn't lose each other."

● Tie all the ropes together and show the audience your long piece of rope with two knots in it. Continue with the story....

● "When they reached the watering hole, the mommy elephant separated her trunk, but no matter how hard she tugged, she couldn't separate the daddy and baby elephants' trunks."

● With the loop still in place, transfer the two ropes to your left hand. With your right hand, bring one end of the long rope up to one end of the short one and hold them together. Then let go of your left hand.

● Show one long piece of rope and say, "The mommy elephant decided to fold the trunk, but that still didn't work. The daddy elephant's trunk had stretched and the baby elephant's trunk was nowhere to be seen."

● "The daddy elephant's trunk was so long that every animal in the jungle was going to trip up on it, so the mommy elephant decided to roll the trunk up. Lo and behold, suddenly the baby elephant's trunk appeared."

● Show the audience the three ropes at their original lengths and say, "Then the mommy elephant realised she was dreaming because the trunks had all reverted back to their original size."

join long and short end ▶ show one long rope ▶ tuck in the long rope end ▶ show the three ropes ■

the three elephants—the secrets

To help you see behind the scenes, we have substituted a blue rope for the smallest rope. When you perform the trick, however, you will need to use the same color for all three pieces of rope.

● When you pick up the end of the baby elephant's trunk, the audience assumes you are placing it next to the other rope/trunk ends.

● In actual fact, you are weaving it behind the long piece of rope and putting it between the long and the middle rope ends. Next, take the dangling end of the middle rope to the right of all the other ropes ends.

● Take the dangling end of the long rope and put it to the right of all the other rope ends, at the base of your thumb. All the rope ends should be held flat in a line so the audience sees six neat rope ends above your hand.

● Keeping the rope ends carefully in place, take the three ends toward your left into your left hand, and pull them apart from your right. The smallest rope has created a loop that makes this possible.

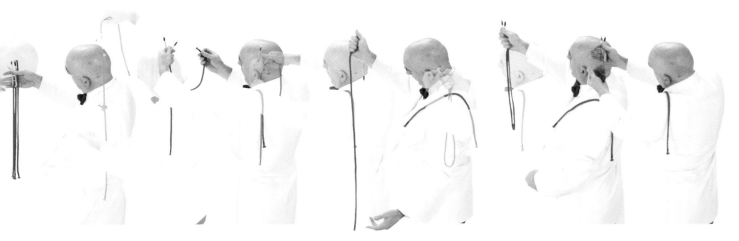

● Your right palm covers the loop as you drop the rope ends in your left hand. From the audience's view, all the ropes appear to be the same length. When you tie the ropes together, the small rope ties around the long rope.

● Untie the genuine knot first and place the middle-length rope over your shoulder. Next, untie the fake knot, making sure your palm obscures from the audience's view the loop created by the short rope.

● When you say you are folding the rope in half, tuck the end of the long rope and the center of the short rope into your fist. The two ends showing at the top of your hand are actually the ends of the short rope.

● From the bottom, wind up and conceal the long rope in your left hand. When you reach your right hand, open both hands to reveal the true lengths of each rope.

show ropes in right hand ▶ **untie the knot** ▶ ▶ **wind up the rope** ■

table top magic

vanishing salt shaker

In this trick, a salt shaker disappears from the top of a table, and then mysteriously reappears in your lap.

- Introduce yourself and the name of your trick to your audience. To perform this trick, you will need a salt shaker, a coin, and a napkin.

- Explain to your audience you are going to cover the salt shaker with your napkin.

- Bring the center of the napkin over the salt shaker, and hold it firmly around the shaker so its shape imprints into the napkin.

- With your left hand, pick up the coin you have left on the table. Tell the audience you are about to tap the salt shaker with the coin; then tap the coin on top of the salt shaker three times.

● Now bring the audience's attention to the coin—hold it up in the air and say you are going to make it magically pass through the table.

● Place the coin on top of the napkin. You need to grip the napkin firmly so it retains the shape of the salt shaker and will also hold the coin.

● Now bring your outstretched palm down hard and fast onto the coin. The napkin will flatten and the noise will surprise the audience. At the same time, pick up the salt shaker from your lap with your other hand.

● Pick up the coin from the table top and voice your dismay. At the same time, tap the shaker underneath the bottom of the table and wonder aloud what the noise is. Then, to the audience's surprise, reveal the shaker.

lap the salt shaker ▶ **place coin on top** ▶ **bang your hand down** ▶ **reveal coin and shaker** ■

vanishing salt shaker—the secrets

Lapping requires very good timing—you need to slide the item toward you and drop it off the edge of the table without the audience seeing what you are doing. Practice the technique well!

● Make sure you hold the napkin at its center when you bring it over the salt shaker. This will make sure it gets completely covered.

● When you tap the coin over the top of the salt shaker, the audience should be able to hear an audible clinking sound.

● After the third tap, bring your left hand swiftly towards the edge of the table. Keep talking to your audience as you draw their attention to the coin – tell them you are going to make it slide through the table.

● Continue to distract your audience, asking them to watch the coin very closely. As you do so, drop the shaker into your lap.

■ **wrap the napkin** ▶ **tap the coin** ▶ **slide shaker to edge** ▶ **drop shaker into lap** ▶

● Bring the napkin back to the center of the table. It will retain its shape if you exert the right amount of pressure on it. The audience won't notice that the salt shaker is no longer underneath the napkin.

● Now carefully place the coin on top of the napkin shape. It should balance there for a few seconds, but no more, so be quick to perform the next move.

● Bring your hand down hard and fast onto the coin and napkin so the napkin crumples into a heap. Reach under the table, picking up the salt shaker from your lap in the process, and tap it under the table.

● Bring the salt shaker up onto the table to reveal that it—rather than the coin—has magically gone through the table.

▶ **balance the coin**   ▶ **bang your hand down**   ▶ **reveal the shaker**

producing a rabbit

This classic crowd pleaser, involving a rabbit appearing from an empty box, is a trick that almost everyone has seen performed at some time.

● Place your magic box on the table in front of you and tell your audience you are going to produce a toy rabbit out of it.

● Undo the clasp at the top of the box to open the top.

● Now undo the clasp at the front to open the front. Tell your audience they are seeing an empty box.

● Now slowly close the top lid and fasten it, and do the same with the side lid. Continue your running commentary on your actions.

■ **present the magic box**　　　**open the top lid**　▶　　**present empty box**　▶　　**close up both sides**　▶

the secrets

● For a fun touch, use a carrot as your magic wand and gently tap the top of the box. Tell your audience you have a much higher rate of success when you use a carrot.

● Slowly open the top lid of the magic box and act surprised as you pull out the toy rabbit.

● Make sure you have put the toy rabbit in the box's secret compartment before you start.

● The box has a mirror inside angled at 45 degrees to reflect the pattern of the box. This gives the illusion of depth, when in fact there is none.

cast magic wand ▶ **pull out soft toy** ■

three cup challenge

No matter how hard they try, no one will ever be able to turn the cups so they face the same way.

● Tell your audience that the test is to twist two cups at once so that, in three turns, all of them face the right way up. Start with the cups lined up as above.

● Take hold of the right-hand cup and the middle cup, and turn them upside down on the spot.

● Keep your eyes focused on the cups as you turn them over.

● Now, take hold of the two outside cups and turn them upside on the spot as well.

■ **explain the aim** ▶ **turn once** ▶ **turn again** ▶

the secret

● Take hold of the middle and right-hand cup again and turn them over. Make sure the sequence occurs quickly and smoothly.

● In three movements you will have managed to make all three cups face up the right way.

● Now, quickly turn the middle cup over and ask a volunteer from the audience to try to replicate your magic movements.

● Unfortunately, they will never be able to do it because the combination you present to them—two facing upright and one facing down—makes it impossible!

present the finish　　▶　　reshuffle the cups　　■　　two facing up

coins through the table 1

In this trick, four coins magically pass through a solid table, and no trap door is required!

● Explain to the audience that you have four coins in your right hand and that, one by one, you will make them go through the table.

● Throw the coins from your right hand to your left, proving that there are four coins.

● Once you have caught them, show the four coins in the palm of your left hand.

● Spread them onto the table for all to see, then pick them up with your right hand.

● Slam all four coins down onto the table. Look at the audience as if to say, "Well, has it worked?"

● Lift your right hand to reveal there are now only three coins. Then, with your left hand, tap under the table with the coin that has passed through.

● Bring your left hand up from under the table to show the coin that has magically passed through the table. Place it to your left. The other three coins are now on top of the table to the right.

● Pick up the three coins in your right hand. With your left hand, pick up the coin that has passed through and take it under the table. Slam the three coins in your right hand down onto the table.

slam down four coins ▶ **tap under the table** ▶ **present the coin** ▶ **take coin under table** ▶

coins through the table 2

To perform this trick well, you need to develop a good rhythm. It is a bit like juggling, so practice well before you perform!

- Lift your right hand to show that there are now only two coins. Next, bring two coins from under table with your left hand and place them on the table.

- Now that you have shown two coins have passed through the table, pick them up with your left hand.

- Take your left hand back under the table, holding the two coins that have passed through, and pick up the two remaining coins in your right hand.

- Slam your right hand down as before, and lift it up to reveal that yet another coin has gone through the table.

the secrets

● Tap under the table with the coins in your left hand, then bring your hand up on top of the table to reveal there are now three coins! Pick up the three coins in your left hand and take them under the table.

● Pick up the last coin with your right hand and slam it down. Lift your hand to show that it, too, has passed through the table. Bring your left hand up to show that all four coins have passed through the table. That's magic!

● Start with five coins in your left hand and only toss four of them to your right hand. Lap the fifth coin. When you pick up the coins, finger palm one of them so it is hidden between your thumb and index finger.

● Each time, lap the palmed coin, and pick up one from your lap to tap underneath the table. The last time, pretend to pick up the last coin but lap it instead.

present three coins   ▶   **slam your right hand down**   ■

cups and balls 1 *magic*

This is a very old trick, and most professional magicians have a variation of it in their routine.

Make sure you use identical cups and balls.

● Tell your audience that you have lined up in front of you a row of three cups and three balls. Now tell your audience that you are going to stack the cups up in one pile.

● Pick up the cup on your left and put it on top of the cup in the middle of the row. Then take the cup on your right and put it on top of the pile.

● Now tell the audience you are going to unstack the cups. Start by placing the top one upside down behind the ball to your right. Make your movements quick and smooth.

● Finish by placing the last cup upside down behind the ball on your left. Talk your audience through your actions.

stack the cups ▶ **unstack the cups** ▶ ▶

● Once you have finished unstacking the cups, pick up the ball in front of the cup on your left.

● Gently place this ball on top of the cup that is in the middle of your row. Make sure it is sitting securely so it doesn't roll away.

● Now tell your audience that you are going to stack the cups up again. Start by taking the cup on your left and placing it on top of the cup in the middle.

● Next, pick up the cup on your right and place it on top to finish stacking the pile.

cups and balls 2 *magic*

The key to this trick is to remember the order of stacking and unstacking the cups. You will have to practice it well if you don't want to get muddled up in mid-trick!

● Explain to your audience that, with a magic tap of the hands, you are now going to make the ball fall through the middle cup to reach the table.

● As you lift up the stack of cups, you will be able to reveal, to the amazement of your audience, a ball underneath the last cup!

● Tell your audience there is more magic to come, and begin to unstack the cups from your right to left. You will need to tilt the stack toward you so it is lying horizontal.

● Take the cup at the bottom of the pile and place it behind the ball farthest to your right. Move the middle cup quickly over the ball to your left.

▶   ▶   **tilt the stack horizontally**   ▶   **unstack the cups**   ▶

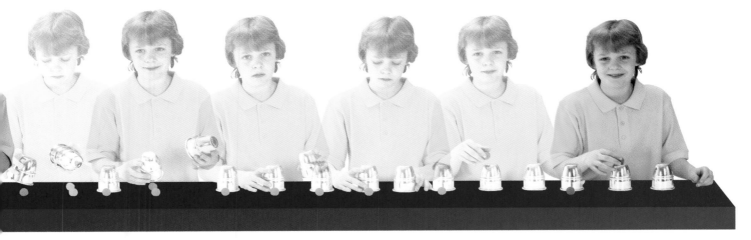

● Place the last cup behind the ball farthest to your left. The cups are now all facing, rim down, in a neat row across the table.

● Next, pick up the ball in front of the middle cup and carefully balance it on top of the cup.

● Now pick up the cup farthest to your left and put it over the middle cup, which has the ball on top.

● Next, take the cup on your right and stack it on top so you now have three cups stacked up in front of you.

▶ **put the ball on the cup** ▶ **stack the cups again** ▶ ▶

Once you find your rhythm and remember the order, you'll be able to do this trick without thinking.

● Tell your audience you are now going to give the top of the stack a magic tap with your hand so the ball will pass through the cup.

● When you pick up the stack, there will be two balls beneath the last cup—the ball has magically passed through the bottom of the middle cup!

● Now unstack the cups as before; tilt the stack and remove from bottom to top, placing them right to left across the table.

● Pick up the last ball in front of the cup to your right. Balance it on top of the cup in the middle of the row.

▶ **tap the top**   **reveal two balls** ▶   **unstack the cups** ▶   **balance ball on middle cup** ▶

the secrets

● Now stack the cups again as before; pick up the cup from your left and stack it over the middle cup with the ball on top first, followed by the cup on your right.

● Cast your magic by tapping the top of the stack with your hands. Pick up the stack to reveal three balls. You have created the illusion that the ball has passed through again.

● In the beginning, set up the cups and balls so that an extra ball is hidden inside the middle cup. This will give the illusion that the ball has passed through the cup.

● Whenever you turn over the cup that hides the extra ball, you must be quick so it doesn't roll out and reveal itself to the audience.

stack the cups again ▶ **reveal three balls** ■

acrobatic matchbox

A matchbox stands up in your hand and opens by itself.

● Clasp your hands in front of you, keeping your elbows bent. Your left hand is concealing the magic matchbox.

● Tell the audience you have a box of matches in your pocket. Put your right hand into your jacket pocket and pull out an identical box of matches. Show it to the audience, then pretend to put it in your left hand.

● As you bring the matches toward your left hand, slide the box into your right palm with your right thumb, concealing it from the audience's view. Point toward your left hand to direct your audience's gaze there.

● Open up your left hand to show the magic box of matches. At the same time, discreetly put the other box of matches back into your right jacket pocket with your right hand.

the secret

● Tell the audience you are plucking a magic hair from your head and are going to use that to cast your magic.

● Now mime the action of tying the magic hair around the matchbox a couple of times and pulling it upward. As you pull the imaginary hair up, gradually push out your left arm and the box rises up onto its side.

● The more you push out with your arm, the more the box will rise. Push slowly until the inner box rises up from the outer cover to reveal the matches inside. Declare it magic.

● The effect is achieved by attaching an invisible nylon thread to the matchbox, running it through your bent jacket sleeve, and attaching it to the other end of your shirt with a safety pin.

▶ **cast a magic spell** ▶ **time your movements** ■

torn and restored paper

This is quite a complicated trick that requires a lot of hand movement behind the scenes (see pages 76–77). Practice in front of a mirror to get an idea of the audience's view.

● Explain to the audience that you are going to fold a large piece of paper into small bits.

● Join the edges of the paper together so you make a crease down the middle. Tear along the crease.

● Hold up the two pieces of torn paper so the audience can see they are clearly separate from each other.

● Place the torn pieces of paper on top of each other, then fold and crease down the middle again.

● Tear the papers in two. The audience will now think you have four ripped pieces of paper.

● Repeat the procedure again; overlap the torn pieces of paper and tear down the middle.

● Now tell your audience that you are going to lock in the papers together, say a special magic word, and restore them into one piece.

● With a dramatic flick of the wrists, your torn pieces of paper will be revealed to the audience as a single sheet of paper again.

tear down the middle ▶ **fold and tear** ▶ **flick your wrists**

torn and restored paper—the secrets

We have shown the two papers in different colors so you can see how the trick works. When you perform it for real, however, you need to use two pieces of paper the same color. The hidden paper will be held together with a magnet, and you will need to practice holding your thumb against it.

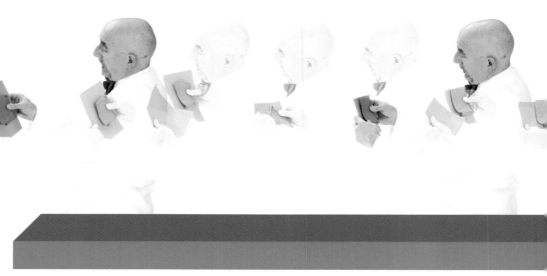

● Behind the large sheet of paper is another piece of paper folded up into nine squares. This is sandwiched between another single sheet of paper, cut to the same size as the final size of the torn-up pieces.

● The single sheet of paper and the folded piece of paper have a small magnet taped to them. Use your thumb to hold them firmly behind the large piece of paper that is showing to the audience.

● As you fold and tear up the large paper, shuffle the smaller papers behind it so they remain hidden from the audience's view.

● By the time you have folded and torn the large, visible paper three times (shown here in green), it will be almost the same size as the hidden folded paper (shown here in blue).

● As you tell your audience you are going to "lock in the papers," you need to take the prefolded piece of paper to the front. The torn pieces of paper are now sandwiched between the single sheet and the folded sheet.

● Make sure you align the magnets on the prefolded piece of paper and the single piece so they can hold the torn pieces together between them. Your fingers will be very busy behind the scenes!

● With the torn papers held firmly in place against the prefolded piece, make a great gesture of unfolding the prefolded paper. Present that to the audience as your restored paper.

▶ **shuffle papers back to front** ▶ **align the magnets** ▶ **unfold prefolded paper** ∎

dollars and oranges 1

A dollar bill jumps from under a cloth to reappear in an orange.

● Ask a member of the audience to volunteer a dollar bill for you to use in your trick. Ask them to read out the last three digits of its registration number (at the bottom left-hand corner) before handing the bill over.

● Roll up the dollar bill tightly with both hands. Hold it in your right hand as you pick up the table napkin in your left hand.

● Now tell the audience you are going to cover the bill with the napkin. Fold the napkin over the rolled dollar bill. Keep the shape of the bill at the top of the napkin.

● Hold the napkin in one hand and hand it back to the volunteer. Ask them to confirm that they can feel the dollar bill.

● Now pick up an orange from a bowl of oranges you have kept at the side of your table.

● Place it down in front of you, and then pick up two more, so you have three lined up in front of you.

● Using the Magician's Force, (see page 8) ask a member of the audience to select the orange in the middle.

● Put the other oranges away to the side of the table, and pick up a small paring knife.

dollars and oranges 2

When you reveal the dollar bill inside the orange, match the audience's amazement with some surprised facial expressions of your own!

● Slowly, and rather dramatically for effect, make a slice at the top of the orange.

● Now tilt the orange slightly toward the audience so the slice you have just made is facing them.

● Use your fingers to break wide open the orange to reveal the rolled up dollar bill.

● As you unroll the bill, read out the last three digits. It will match those on the dollar bill hidden inside the napkin. The audience will be amazed!

▶ cut into the orange   tilt the orange   ▶   break open thea bill   ▶   confirm the bill is the original ■

the secrets

This trick requires deft hand movements, so practice well before you

perform it in front of an audience.

● Cut a hole in the bottom of an orange a few hours before the show, and leave it to dry. Place the doctored orange in the middle and use the Magician's Force (see page 8) so it will be chosen.a

● Slide a rolled-up dollar bill into the seam of the napkin. When you take the dollar bill from the audience, they will think that it is the one they can feel in the napkin.

● After you have put the bill behind the napkin, quickly push it back into your right palm. Cup your hand so it stays there but is hidden from view.

● When you pick up the doctored orange, push the bill into its hole.

cut hole in orange ▶ **hide bill in napkin seam** ▶

sponge ball routine 1

Produce three balls from thin air, and then make them travel, one by one, through a solid bowl.

● Start the routine by holding your arms out, elbows slightly bent and palms facing the audience, proving that you have nothing concealed.

● Bring your right hand over to your left forearm and pull up your jacket sleeve so the audience can see there is nothing hidden up your arm. Do the same on the other side.

● Bring your hands together and make a rubbing motion. A ball suddenly appears from thin air. Put it down on the table in front of you.

● Pick up this magic ball and smile at the audience.

● Show the audience the ball by holding it with both palms. Push the ball into one hand.

● Rub your palms together a couple of times. As you slowly separate your hands, one ball has now become two balls. Place the balls on the table in front of you.

● Draw the audience's attention to the sponge balls on the table by steadying them with your right hand, then pick them both up.

● Rub your hands together and when you release them, the audience will see that the two balls have now become three balls.

hold the ball up to audience ▶ **reveal two balls** ▶ **pick up a third ball** ▶ **reveal three balls** ▶

sponge ball routine 2

As the trick continues, the three balls will magically pass through a solid bowl.

● Pick up a bowl with your right hand or, if you have an assistant, ask them to hand over a bowl from the right side. Show the audience the inside of the bowl to prove it is empty.

● Place the bowl on the table behind the line of the three balls. Pick up the ball farthest to your left and tell the audience you are making a well in your left hand.

● Poke the ball deep into your closed left fist with your index finger. Lay your left hand down flat on the table.

● Tell the audience that you are now going to "sprinkle" the ball through the bowl. Pick up the bowl with your right hand—the ball has magically travelled through the bowl and is underneath.

▶ **show the inside of the bowl** ▶   **place the bowl face down**   ▶   ▶   **sprinkle the ball**   ▶

● As the audience marvels, transfer the bowl to your right hand and place it back over the ball. Pick up the second (middle) ball and poke it into your left hand.

● Palm and sprinkle the ball, as before. Pick up the bowl to reveal that the second ball has travelled through the solid bowl.

● Pick up the third ball. At the same time, show the audience that the bowl is empty.

● Place the bowl over the two balls. Hold the third ball on your open palm. You are not going to sprinkle the ball through. Instead, quickly slam it on top of the bowl.

sponge ball routine 3

In the finale of this trick, you will now turn a single sponge ball into an orange and a lemon.

● Lift the bowl to show the audience it is empty. Pick up the three balls with your left hand and put them in your pocket.

● Show the bowl again, proving that there is nothing concealed, then place it on the table. Take one sponge ball from your pocket and poke it into your hand as before.

● Sprinkle over the bowl, lift the bowl to reveal the sponge ball underneath. Put the sponge ball back into your pocket.

● Put the bowl back down, then quickly pick it up again. There is now an orange underneath. Place the orange to one side and put the bowl back down again. Quickly pick it up to reveal a lemon.

▶   ▶   **poke ball**   ▶   ▶   **reveal orange, then lemon**   ▶

the secrets

The key stages behind performing the routine are shown below.
The routine should be performed smoothly and quickly, almost
like a juggling act, so make sure you practice well beforehand.

● Hide a ball in the elbow crease of your jacket before you start the first routine. You will need to keep both arms slightly bent. When you tug your sleeves, pick up the first ball and conceal it in your hand.

● Draw the audience's attention to the single ball on the table while you take a second ball out from your pocket. Squeeze the two together when you pick up the second one—it will still look like one.

● When you seem to be poking the ball into your fist, you are actually performing the French Drop (see page 12). The hidden ball is pressed against the inside of the bowl. It is released when the bowl is put down.

● Misdirect the audience, then under the cover of the bowl, load the lemon and orange from your pocket.

hide ball in jacket   ■   **squeeze two balls together**   ■

that's a smashing watch 1

This trick makes a dramatic finish to your magic show—especially to those members of the audience who have offered up their personal possessions! It requires practice, since it involves many props.

● Present a table napkin rolled up in a napkin ring and introduce yourself to your audience.

● Carefully pull the napkin out of the holder. Hold its top corners and shake the napkin out in front of you with both hands.

● Turn the napkin into a diamond shape, holding the top corner with your left hand. With your other hand, bring the opposite corner up to the corner you are holding.

● Now bring the corners at the sides of the triangle up to the corner you are holding in your right hand. You should now be holding all the corners in one hand.

● Now ask members of the audience to hand you small items such as coins, rings, and keys. Drop them inside the first fold so they lie in the pouch of the napkin.

● Each time you drop an item, shake the napkin so the audience can hear the items inside.

● Ask a member of the audience to volunteer a watch.

● Drop the watch into the napkin and draw attention to it with your free hand.

drop items in first fold ▶   **shake pouch to make noise** ▶   **lay napkin down on table** ▶

that's a smashing watch 2

It's good to create a lot of noise when you bang down with the mallet, but be careful not to bang too hard—you don't want to mark the table!

● Ask your assistant to pass you your mallet. Show that it is a solid weight by lifting it up and bringing it down into your hand.

● Take the mallet up and over your shoulder to get a good swing on it.

● Bring the mallet down hard and fast onto the edge of the napkin, away from its center.

● Next, put the mallet away and pick up the napkin from the corners. Shake it so the audience can clearly hear the smashed contents.

▶ **hold up mallet** ▶ **slam the mallet down** ▶ ▶

● Unravel the napkin and hold it up from its center so the contents fall onto the table.

● Pick out the (unscathed) personal items, such as keys, rings, and coins, and return them to their owners.

● As you pick up the bits of the broken watch, be prepared for the shock on the unhappy owner's face!

● Immediately reassure the watch owner, however, by saying that you have an idea....

reveal the contents ▷ **return items to audience** ▷ **reveal broken watch** ▷

that's a smashing watch 3

When you reveal the smashed watch to the audience, don't dwell on its broken contents for too long. Its owner will be very eager for you to restore it!

● Explain to the audience that you are going to sweep the contents of the broken watch into your hand.

● Now take the napkin with your right hand and hold it up high in front of you.

● Put your left hand, which is holding the broken watch pieces, into your jacket pocket.

● Drop the napkin to reveal the restored watch. Check that it is working and return it, with thanks, to its owner.

the secrets

You will need to take apart a watch and place its contents in the secret pocket sewn on the inside of the napkin.

● Buy a cheap watch and take it apart. Put its pieces into the pocket you have sewn at one of the corners of the napkin. The opening of the pocket should face the corner.

● The napkin needs to be folded as per the instructions; this creates special folds and pockets. When you put an item in the first fold, it falls into the pouch; when you put in the second fold, it will fall through.

● When the watch falls, move back slightly. Let the watch fall onto your lap. Continue to direct the audience's attention to the top of the napkin.

● Behind the screen of the napkin, swap the pieces of watch for the real watch in your lap.

dismantle a cheap watch ▷ **fold the napkin carefully** ▷ **lap the watch** ▷

index

A

Acrobatic Matchbox 72–73
Appearing and Disappearing Cards 26–29
appearing tricks
    Appearing and Disappearing Cards 26–29
    Cups and Balls 66–71
    palms and sleights 10–12, 65
        Producing a Rabbit 58–59
        Sponge Ball Routine 82–87
arm movement 36–37
arranging card decks 21, 23, 25
audiences
    misdirecting 12, 20–21, 32, 41, 60–61, 87
    props from 78–79, 88–89
    talking to 16–17, 36–37, 46–49, 58, 66–69
    volunteers 20–24, 30–33, 40–41, 43, 61, 88–93

B

balls 66–71
    from thin air 82–83, 87
    palming 10
    through a bowl 84–86
bowls 82–87
boxes 26–29, 58–59
broken watch 90

C

card tricks 14–33
    Appearing and Disappearing Cards 26–29
    Forcing a Card 24–25
    Four Burglars 16–17

    Fun With Letters 9
    palming a card 11
    Rising Card 30–33
    Suspended Cards 18–19
    Top Card Turnover 22–23
    Turn the Card Over 20–21
children 7
    audiences 20
    palming a card 11
cloth 40–41, 54–57, 78–81, 88
coins 54–57, 62–65
    palming 10, 12
Coins Through the Table 62–65
concealment 10
concentration 7
counting tricks 8–9
cups 60–61, 66–71

Cups and Balls 66–71
Cut and Restored Rope 42–45

D

defying gravity 18–19
dexterity 7, 32
disappearing tricks
    Appearing and Disappearing

Cards 26–29
Coins Through the Table 62–65
French Drop 12, 87
palms and sleights 10–12, 65
Sponge Ball Routine 82–87
Vanishing Salt Shaker 54–57
distracting the audience
by talking 36–37, 66–69
eye contact 20–21, 32, 41
eye movement 12, 60
misdirection 12, 60–61, 87
Dollars and Oranges 78–81

E
equipment
balls 10, 66–71, 82–87
bowls 82–87
boxes 26–29
broken watch 90
cloth 40–41, 54–57, 78–81, 88
coins 10, 12, 54–57, 62–65
cups 60–61, 66–71
from the audience 78–79, 88–89
glue 28
handkerchiefs 25
knives 79–80
magic boxes 58–59
magnets 76–77
mallets 90
matchboxes 72–73
miniature cards 11
mirrors 58–59, 74
needle 36–37
nylon thread 73
paper 74–77

preparation 19, 25, 28
rabbit 58–59
rings 40–41
rope tricks 36, 40, 46
salt shakers 54–57
scissors 42
sponge balls 10, 82–87
eye contact 20–21, 32, 41
eye movement 12, 60

F
fanning cards 16–17, 18–19, 20–21
finger skills 32–33, 36, 44–45
palming 10, 65
Flowmotion system 13
folding cloth 93
Forcing a Card 24–25
Four Burglars 16–17
French Drop 12, 87
Fun With Letters 9

G
glue 28
gravity, defying 18–19

H
hand movement 36–37, 39, 42–45, 74–77, 81
palms and sleights 10–12, 51, 65
handkerchiefs 25
helpers 20–24, 30–33, 40–41, 43, 61, 88–93

I
It's a Snip 42–45

J
juggling acts 36, 64, 87

K
knives 79–80
knots 38–39, 40–41, 44–45, 48–49

L
lapping 11, 54–57, 65, 93

M
magic boxes 26–29, 58–59
magic words 19, 21, 75
Magician's Force 81
see also Forcing a Card
magnets 76–77
mallets 90
matchboxes 72–73
mime 73
miniature cards 11
mirrors 58–59, 74
misdirection 12, 60–61, 87
movement 10–12, 36–39, 42–45, 74–77, 81

N
napkins see cloth
needles 36–37
nylon thread 73

P
palms 10–12, 51, 65

paper 74–77
performance tips
see also audiences
juggling acts 36, 64, 87
lapping 11, 54–57, 65, 93
movement 10–12, 36–37, 38–39, 42–45, 74–77, 81
palming 10–12, 51, 65
presentation 7
rhythm 64, 68–70, 87
showmanship 40
storytelling 16–17, 46–49, 58
talking to audience 36–37, 66–69
timing 56–57
playing cards see card tricks
prediction tricks 8–9
Fun With Letters 9
Sweet Trick 8–9
preparation
arranging card decks 21, 23, 25
card tricks 19, 25, 28
table top magic 71, 72–73, 76–77, 81, 93
presentation 7
Producing a Rabbit 58–59
professional magicians 7
Professor's Nightmare 46–47
props see equipment

Q
Quick Release Ring 40–41

R
rabbits 58–59
restored rope 42–45

rhythm 64, 68–70, 87
rings, solid 40–41
Rising Card 30–33
rope tricks 34–51
    It's a Snip 42–45
    Professor's Nightmare 46–47
    Quick Release Ring 40–41
    Self-Tying Knots 38–39
    Thread Needle 36–37
    Three elephants 46–51

S

salt shakers 54–57
scissors 42
self improvement 7
Self-Tying Knots 38–39
showmanship 40
sleights 10–12
solid rings 40–41
spelling tricks 8–9
Sponge Ball Routine 82–87
sponge balls 10, 82–87
storytelling 16–17, 46–49, 58
Suspended Cards 18–19
Sweet Trick 8–9

T

table top magic 52–93
    Acrobatic Matchbox 72–73
    Coins Through the Table 62–65
    Cups and Balls 66–71
    Dollars and Oranges 78–81
    French Drop 87
    Producing a Rabbit 58–59
    Sponge Ball Routine 82–87
    That's a Smashing Watch 88–93
    Three Cup Challenge 60–61
    Torn and Restored Paper 74–77
    Vanishing Salt Shaker 54–57
talking to audience 36–37, 66–69
    see also storytelling
That's a Smashing Watch 88–93
Thread Needle 36–37
Three Cup Challenge 60–61
Three elephants 46–51
timing 56–57
Top Card Turnover 22–23
Torn and Restored Paper 74–77
Turn the Card Over 20–21
tying knots 38–39, 40–41, 44–45,
    48–49

V

Vanishing Salt Shaker 54–57
volunteers 20–24, 30–33, 40–41, 43,
    61, 88–93

W

watch, smashing 88–93